# ISO22301

A Pocket Guide

# ISO22301

## A Pocket Guide

TONY DREWITT

IT Governance Publishing

Every possible effort has been made to ensure that the information contained in this book is accurate at the time of going to press, and the publishers and the author cannot accept responsibility for any errors or omissions, however caused. Any opinions expressed in this book are those of the author, not the publisher. Websites identified are for reference only, not endorsement, and any website visits are at the reader's own risk. No responsibility for loss or damage occasioned to any person acting, or refraining from action, as a result of the material in this publication can be accepted by the publisher or the author.

IT Governance Publishing
IT Governance Limited
Unit 3, Clive Court
Bartholomew's Walk
Cambridgeshire Business Park
Ely
Cambridgeshire
CB7 4EA
United Kingdom
www.itgovernance.co.uk

© Tony Drewitt 2013

First published in the United Kingdom in 2013 by IT Governance Publishing.

ISBN: 978-1-84928-480-6

# CONTENTS

# INTRODUCTION

This pocket guide is intended to meet the needs of two groups:

1 Individual readers who have turned to it as an introduction to a topic that they know little about.

2 Organisations implementing, or considering implementing, a business continuity plan and management system.

In either case, this guide furnishes readers with an understanding of the basics of business continuity, including:

- A definition of what business continuity means.
- How managing operational business continuity risk can be achieved using an approach increasingly recognised worldwide.
- The important distinction between operational, commercial and strategic risks in business.
- The role played by operational resilience measures, business continuity strategies and planning in managing operational risks.
- How to demonstrate some form of return on investment in a business continuity management system (BCMS).
- The role of business continuity in corporate governance and how to develop a mechanism that provides directors and stakeholders with appropriate assurance about the management and control of business continuity risks.

Corporate bodies will find this pocket guide useful at a number of stages in any business continuity project, including:

- At the decision-making stage; to ensure that those committing to a business continuity programme do so from a truly informed position.

- At project initiation stage; as an introduction to business continuity for the board, project team members and those on the periphery of the project.
- As part of an ongoing awareness campaign, being made available to all staff[1] and to new starters as part of their introduction to the company.

Corporate users may find they get the most benefit from making this pocket guide available to staff and adding a small flyer inside it which explains how it relates to their own specific environment, or where they are addressed in their business continuity management system.

The guide is designed to be read without having to frequently break from the text, but there is a short list of abbreviations, terms and definitions in Chapter 7. Also available from IT Governance is a glossary containing a comprehensive collection of relevant definitions.[2] The footnotes are not essential reading, and if you are new to the subject it is recommended you ignore them on your first read-through; they will be of more relevance on a second reading, particularly if you are involved in a business continuity project or in decision-making at any stage of a BCM project.

On finishing your initial read-through it is suggested you keep a copy for easy reference.

A word of warning: this is not an implementation or 'how to do it' guide.

---

[1] Why not conduct sample surveys of people's understanding of some aspects of business continuity and compile the results to demonstrate the effectiveness of your awareness campaign? Results can be used as a contribution to the *performance evaluation* section of the standard for a management review. See ISO22301:2012 section 9.

[2] *Business Continuity and BS25999: A Combined Glossary* (ITGP, 2008), available from www.itgovernance.co.uk.

Implementing an ISO22301-compliant BCMS requires more advice than a Pocket Guide, such as this is designed to offer. A BCMS project is, in most cases, likely to equate to a significant business change project, and will require all the project governance arrangements that suit such an undertaking.

# CHAPTER 1: BUSINESS CONTINUITY – WHAT'S THAT?

In any organisational endeavour, be it a business, a public body or a not-for-profit organisation, the basic premise is that it does what it does without being interrupted by unforeseen factors. In order to do this, all organisations must continue to have available to them all of the resources and services upon which they depend, and must be allowed to continue doing what they do.

## Resources

As they evolve, most businesses and other organisations acquire the resources upon which they depend. If any of these critical resources are lost or are taken away, the organisation is likely to find itself in trouble.

Most organisations have some contingencies for certain resource failures (usually in their IT systems) but these are often patchy and based on an individual's intuitive estimate of what level of resource would actually be required, and when.

Today, virtually all organisations rely upon common resource types, including:

- IT systems
- paper records
- telecommunications
- people
- workplace(s)
- money.

Many others rely additionally on other, more specifically physical, resources, such as:

- plant and equipment
- vehicles

- logistics
- specialised storage, handling and processing facilities.

## Licence to operate

Most businesses are allowed to do what they do provided they operate within the law. On the other hand, many public bodies and an increasing number of businesses (for example, in the financial sector) operate under some form of licence, permission or authority which could, under certain circumstances, be withdrawn.

For many, this can be considered an operational (and therefore a business continuity) risk, particularly where only some of the organisation's activities are licensed or regulated.

Critically, each organisation must decide, as a matter of policy, whether risks associated with its licence to operate should be included within the scope of their business continuity management system.

Policy and scope are described in more detail in Chapter 4.

## The key deliverable – the business continuity plan

Almost anyone can write a document called a business continuity plan (BCP), but there is no purpose in doing so if it doesn't deliver what is actually required when a disaster or business-interrupting incident or situation occurs.

This pocket guide doesn't review the many ways in which most BCPs are not actually fit for purpose; the reality is that, in comparison to modern best-practice standards for business continuity management, most organisations' BCPs will prove horribly inadequate. This guide looks at how ISO22301 can help to ensure that BCPs do actually deliver what is needed; that they are, in fact, fit for purpose and as a result, can deliver some return on the investment in them.

**Why does business continuity matter?**

Many people regard business continuity as a form of risk management or insurance; a means of ensuring that, if something goes wrong, there is a way of limiting or even eliminating the impact.

This view is largely appropriate; however, there are a number of other important reasons, outlined below, why organisations should have a business continuity management programme.

### Competitive edge

As the risk of suppliers letting them down, due to operational issues, becomes more visible to a growing number of companies and other organisations, those organisations are starting to seek formal assurance that their suppliers will be able to continue supplying them in the event of some interruptive incident. This supply chain dynamic is already used in customers' due diligence processes together with other criteria including financial stability, quality management systems and information security.

The existence of a recognised business continuity standard provides a real benchmark against which organisations can satisfy themselves as to their suppliers' operational resilience. For suppliers, this means that having a BCMS that is compliant with, and better still certified to, ISO22301 can amount to a significant competitive advantage.

### Licence to operate

The loss of a licence to operate represents a risk that could make significant financial impact, so the existence of a BCMS is increasingly becoming a condition of such licences.

For instance, the UK Solicitors' Code of Conduct 2007 includes the requirement for all solicitors to provide for absences and emergencies,[3] and all Category 1 responders under the UK Civil Contingencies Act 2006 are required to have tested business continuity plans. It is, of course, within the spirit of this legislation that the plans in question do actually work. ISO22301 now provides a truly international basis and benchmark for organisations to demonstrate their operational resilience and builds upon its predecessor, BS25999, which was the first real blueprint for business continuity arrangements.

## Insurance

Many organisations have business interruption cover within their business insurance portfolio. This cover will usually compensate the organisation for its loss of profit in the event of an interruption, for a period called the indemnity period. This cover does not, though, compensate for any future business that is lost after this indemnity period, which is often only one or two years.

Business interruption insurance is usually a significant cost; the existence of a BCMS often provides the opportunity to reduce the amount of cover that is needed and, therefore, the insurance premium.

## Corporate governance

Corporate governance is frequently referred to as a reason for 'doing' business continuity, but often without a proper explanation of its significance.

The UK's *Combined Code on Corporate Governance 2003*, the code of Best Practice with which, under The London Stock Exchange Listing Rules, all Stock Exchange-listed companies are required to comply, includes the requirement (*Section C.2.1*) to report that the board has conducted 'a review of the effectiveness of the group's system of internal controls'.

---

[3] Solicitors' Code of Conduct 2007, Rule 5 Clause 5.01 (1) (k) 'the continuation of the practice of the firm in the event of absences and emergencies, with the minimum interruption to clients' business'.

The Turnbull Guidance on Internal Controls (which provides specific guidance on compliance with the Combined Code), whilst focusing significantly on financial controls, is also clear that the organisation must ensure it is able to 'respond appropriately to significant business, operational, financial, compliance and other risks to achieving the company's objectives'.

Whilst neither the letter of the Combined Code nor the Turnbull Guidance state that listed companies or those seeking listing must have a business continuity plan, the spirit of 'responding appropriately', in today's business climate is usually taken to mean that business continuity planning is a basic requirement as part of the organisation's operational risk management and internal control measures.

For privately owned companies and those limited by guarantee, there remains an expectation amongst all stakeholders that boards will also respond appropriately to operational risks, as they do to financial and legislative ones, and that appropriate business continuity arrangements will be in place.

A further issue for directors is that of personal liability. If a major incident occurs and it subsequently transpires that, because of the lack of BCM, certain parties sustain loss or injury, directors could potentially be prosecuted for lack of proper risk assessment.[4]

The best way to provide evidence of appropriate management and control of the operational risks that could lead to business interruption is to develop and implement a BCMS that meets the requirements of ISO22301 and is, preferably, also externally certified against the standard.

---

[4] See *Expecting the Unexpected* (London First, 2003).

# CHAPTER 2: BEFORE BCM

It is in the nature of any new discipline that assumptions tend to be made about what the new 'thing' is, and whether it is necessary or whether it is just another version of something else.

Historically, people involved with running organisations tended to implement risk controls on an *ad hoc* and intuitive basis, responding to changing systems, rather than systematically. Locking doors, for instance, only became common when social change meant that a growing number of people were actually likely to walk into somebody else's house or place of business and steal things.

The genesis of business continuity arguably lies in the introduction of computers to business. The considerable benefits that have derived from the use of computers in speeding up business processes and improving productivity, soon became dulled by the realisation that computers were quite likely to go wrong and that, when they did, this tended to have a significant impact.

So 'disaster recovery' (DR) appeared: services provided initially by computer manufacturers and later by dedicated service providers, to help organisations to restore their computer systems in the event of failure.

It seems clear that this capability to restore resources and processes that support businesses and other organisations can, and should, apply to all resources, not just computers.

For some time, this broader set of capabilities was also referred to as Disaster Recovery (DR), not least because serviced recovery workspace was made available by some of the computer manufacturers who also offered the replacement technology.

## 2: Before BCM

The arrival of BS25999-1 in 2006 and BS25999-2 in 2007 brought a degree of consistency of terminology amongst people engaged in anything to do with business continuity or resilience. The previous edition of this guide (BS25999: A pocket guide) suggested that people might begin to talk the same language, and to some extent that has happened. ISO22301 makes some changes to the BCM lexicon, but generally these make good sense and the true international status of the new standard should help this to progress further.

BCM has evolved over the past 25 years or so and, while not replacing DR, has incorporated it into a much broader, organisation-wide approach to operational resilience.

ISO22301 has continued the exclusion of the term DR and in the author's experience this acronym is used much less today as shorthand for business continuity.

There is also often a temptation to confuse insurance with BCM; to assume that BCM isn't necessary if one has business interruption insurance cover in place. In theory this could almost be true, if one had a business interruption insurance policy with an indefinite indemnity period, no limit of indemnity, and cover for all the severance costs for all employees. Such a policy almost certainly doesn't exist and, if it did, the premium would be crippling.

Insurance remains an important component of any organisation's resilience in the face of operational risks and interruptions, but it should always be seen as complementary to BCM, not as a substitute.

# CHAPTER 3: THE BUSINESS CONTINUITY MANAGEMENT SYSTEM

Chapter 1 refers to the key deliverable of business continuity planning as a business continuity plan that actually works. Every organisation should satisfy itself that its BCP is fit for purpose otherwise the investment in developing the plan will have been wasted.

The BCMS is designed to ensure that the plan is, indeed, fit for purpose. It does this by:

- Understanding and analysing the business recovery requirements, so that the impact resulting from an incident or interruption is properly understood and balanced across the organisation.
- Identifying and planning the resources that would be required in the worst possible situation, and ensuring that they would be available.
- Creating a documented plan that is based upon valid assumptions, delivers the required recovery outcomes and is properly understood, or 'owned', by those that are likely to need to use it.
- Testing the plan, resources and people involved so that everything remains up to date, capabilities are tested and the best level of assurance can be given as to the fitness for purpose of the plan.

These four key components will be well understood by anyone involved in running an organisation. However, a potential weakness in such a system has to do with the fact that the business continuity plan may never be needed. BCM is a contingent discipline and not 'core business' to any organisation except those involved in providing BCM products and services. It is quite likely, therefore, not to get the attention that it requires if it is to be reliable at the point of need.

A comprehensive BCMS therefore goes further than the functional components listed above. It includes policy, commitment and engagement from senior management, creating the 'ownership' throughout the organisation that makes the plans and arrangements operable in practice.

All these aspects were embodied into a code of practice published by BSI in the 1990s called PAS 56. This rather complex document was superseded in 2006 and 2007 by parts 1 and 2, respectively, of BS25999 which continued to feature something called the 'business continuity management lifecycle'.

This 'lifecycle' is really just a way of saying that BCM is a reiterative process, rather than a one-off project. That, of course, is still true however, ISO22301 does not feature the 'lifecycle', instead basing the management process upon the 'plan – do – check – act (PDCA)' model, which is a feature of all ISO management system standards available for accredited certification, and many other standards besides.

The lifecycle was much more discipline specific than the PDCA model; the latter being almost generic across a number of management system standards.

However, ISO22301 does include all of the discipline specific requirements, but they are not set out in the same lifecycle approach.

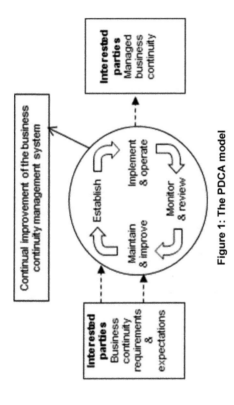

Figure 1: The PDCA model

## CHAPTER 4: ISO22301 – BCMS – REQUIREMENTS

Similar to other standards, ISO22301 devotes its first three sections to Scope, Normative References and Terms & Definitions. The remaining seven sections are summarised as follows:

### 4 Context of the Organisation - establishing and documenting:

- What the organisation does and the potential impact of disruptions
- Relationship with other policies and wider risk management
- Contractual and other requirements
- Who the interested parties are
- Scope of the management system

The standard definitely pushes the boundaries of trust in organisational managers; it is ever so slightly obsessive about repeatedly analysing and documenting what the organisation does. What used to be covered in the 'understanding the organisation' section of BS25999 is now split between this section on context and section 8 on operation.

### 5 Leadership - establishing and documenting:

- Leadership and commitment with respect to BCM
- A BCM Policy
- Roles, responsibilities and authorities

BS25999 included numerous disparate references to the commitment, responsibilities and roles made and taken by the organisation's management. ISO22301 has cleaned up this area quite a lot with an entire section describing the requirements for commitment, including, of resources, policy and roles. Because BCM isn't core business, it is very difficult to implement a BCMS properly without commitment to it at board level and below.

The board needs to understand that we now live in an environment where hoping for the best, 'winging it' and assuming that things will 'just happen' are not acceptable. BCM has evolved as a management discipline because it is the only way of comprehensively managing the risks of business interruption.

The standard looks for the organisation's management to demonstrate commitment, to be involved in the BCMS development process and in the ongoing review of its various components.

One of the best ways of making this commitment 'real' is to establish a Business Continuity Committee, or a Risk Management Committee, with membership from all parts of the organisation.

### *Policy*

In addition to making the commitment to BCM and resourcing the programme, the planning stage should also include the development of a policy.

The policy should be concise and include statements setting out:

- scope
- commitment and intent
- summary objectives for minimising impact, providing continuity to customers and protecting stakeholders.

Where practical, it makes sense to write the policy so that it can be read by any interested party, particularly including employees, but also so that it can be approved by the board, or its equivalent.

A policy is usually a fairly important tool in building awareness within the organisation as well as being how the board tells the executive what it wants; what the BCM and related objectives are.

## 6 Planning - determining and documenting:

- The risks and opportunities presented by the objectives and requirements
- BC objectives and plans to achieve them
- Minimum acceptable levels of output
- Some form of project plan with an evaluation mechanism

In some respects this section overlaps section 4 and continues the analysis of what the organisation does, what its risks therefore are and, hopefully directly related to this, its BCM objectives. It does make sense that minimum acceptable levels of operating are understood here – it would be fair to say that many organisations probably don't understand what their minimum acceptable levels are.

### *Project management*

This section is probably the best place also to include the overall project plan for BCM; though at some point it will need to develop from a project into a process, since BCM is an ongoing, or continuous, process.

Once again, it should be fairly self-evident that, if you are going to have a proper BCMS, you also need a formal project to make it happen. It is usually very difficult to operate a re-iterative PDCA process without a project framework and clearly the practical implications of this are:

- allocation of resources
- someone to perform the role of Business Continuity Manager and, importantly, someone able to dedicate a significant proportion of their time to it during the first year or so.

A classic trap that many organisations fall into is to give BCM responsibility to someone who 'isn't very busy'. What usually happens is that something called a 'Business Continuity Plan' emerges that is not fit for purpose and, if it is ever activated for real, the organisation simply does not recover in the way that all the 'busy' executives had assumed it would.

A good BCM project will be managed by a competent and skilled manager and will feature an appropriate oversight body (the Business Continuity Committee), regular progress and development meetings and, equally importantly, a budget against which costs and savings (**yes, savings!**) can be allocated.

**7 Support - establishing a range of resources that underpin the BCMS, including:**

- A competence system
- An awareness programme
- A communications plan to include both incident and non-incident situations
- Documentation and its management

This is a nice logical section. It describes the key things that any organisation will need to create, maintain and benefit from a good BCMS.

### *Awareness*

Awareness is very significant to the success of BCM. Just as senior managers need to make a real commitment to BCM, everyone else in the organisation should understand it and 'own' it at the appropriate level.

Management commitment may enable the BCMS to be developed, but it is critical that all of the information upon which it is based is current, accurate and understood by people connected with it.

Ultimately, in the event of an incident, many people in the organisation would be required to respond in one way or another and the better their level of awareness of the BCP, the more likely it is that the outcome will be as planned and expected.

One of the best ways to achieve this aim is to make BCM part of individual job descriptions and the individual performance review process.

## 8 Operation - planning and implementing processes that deliver:

- Business impact analysis & risk assessment
- Strategies
- (Contingency) resources
- Impact mitigation
- Incident response structure & plans
- Exercise & test arrangements

### *Business impact analysis*

The premise of the business impact analysis (BIA) is that you need to work out, not guess, how quickly each activity would need to be resumed in the event it is disrupted.

Any number of consultants and possibly some publications suggest a different purpose for the BIA, but the clue to what it really is for is in its title – analysis of impact.

The standard doesn't go into much detail on how to conduct a BIA and neither can this pocket guide[5], except to summarise the principles.

Most organisations already segment their activities in a wide variety of ways. This should make it possible to assess the impact on the organisation if each of these activities is

---

[5] For a complete and detailed description of how to conduct a BIA, see *Business Continuity: A Manager's Guide to ISO22301* by Tony Drewitt (ITGP, 2013).

interrupted, whatever the cause. In the vast majority of cases, impact will increase with time, so an analysis of impacts which allows for variance over time can provide an objective way of establishing what duration of interruption can be tolerated for each activity and for the organisation as a whole.

A key outcome of this analysis is a recovery time objective (RTO) for each activity. The RTO will form the basis of the business continuity plan and, importantly, planning for the provision of interim or DR resources.

All activities depend upon a variety of resources. Another essential element of BIA is to identify these resources so that they can be analysed and fed into the other stages of the BCMS.

Like the rest of BCM, BIA is a recurring activity. The frequency with which BIA reviews should be conducted may sensibly be included in the policy, but the first iteration will naturally be much more resource intensive, as it will include some form of 'mapping' of business processes or activities.

This phase is likely to take a number of months to achieve, dependent upon the size and complexity of the organisation.

BIA may also be linked to a broader operational risk assessment, and ISO22301 identifies ISO31000[6] as an appropriate basis for this. Whilst BCM is essentially about impact rather than likelihood, there is little sense in making provision for some eventuality that is in a lower order of magnitude of probability.

There are a number of approaches to risk management including ISO31000, which does not itself describe how to conduct risk assessment. Instead it refers to ISO31010[7] which doesn't really set out a clear method either. It does, though, emphasis that risk is all about uncertainty and that it is some

---

[6] ISO31000:2009 Risk management – Principles and guidelines
[7] IEC/ISO31010 Risk management – Risk assessment techniques

combination of probability (or likelihood) and impact, often represented by the classic probability/impact matrix, or PIM.

This provides an objective basis for scoring risks that is broadly considered appropriate in corporate governance terms at least.

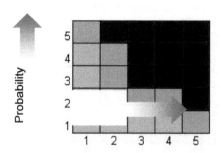

**Figure 2: A typical probability/impact matrix**

In this example, there are five levels of both probability and impact. A classic pitfall is to leave out the definitions of what these levels actually are – the assessment criteria.

Provided that clear criteria are set, a number of suitably capable individuals can assess a variety of operational risks and come up with reproducible and comparable results.

The risk score is simply the product of probability and impact:

**Risk = Probability x Impact**

Broadly speaking, a risk with a probability of 2 and an impact of 4 (score = 8) is seen as the same as one with a probability of 4 and an impact of 2.

Risk score is also often expressed as $P + I + n$, where n can be zero or a –ve or +ve integer. This method gives a similar distribution of scores in a typical matrix.

There is no definitive or statutory method; these are simply approaches used extensively in risk management practice.

It is also useful, for risk treatment purposes, to consider the range of risk scores (between 1 and 25 in the example above) in bands. A common approach here is to use red/amber/green (RAG), where red indicates a high risk and green is low or, if colour is not available, a simple high/medium/low classification.

| Band | From | To |
|------|------|-----|
| H | 9 | 25 |
| M | 5 | 8 |
| L | 1 | 4 |

**Figure 3: Risk score bands**

The selection of these bands is a matter of intuition and can also be described as 'risk appetite', but what is important is the objectivity that is introduced and the consequent opportunity to document and prioritise individual risks for treatment or control.

Probably the most effective way of managing assessed risks is a risk register. This should be a key tool used both by the Business Continuity Manager and the Business Continuity or Risk Committee.

### *Business continuity strategy*

In simple terms, this is about deciding how each activity or group of activities will, or will not, be resumed.

It may seem counter-intuitive to decide not to resume certain activities in the event of interruption. Some organisations may have specific activities which, if suspended during an interim period following an incident and before returning to the original premises or operating state, would have no lasting impact on the business. This could be the case where no customers or, perhaps suppliers, perceive that they have been let down by such a suspension.

However, these cases are generally the exception rather than the rule. Strategy is usually about how to resume the interrupted activity as quickly as possible and within the RTO set for each activity.

This is an area in which savings are possible. Most companies have established their IT DR on an intuitive basis and, whether it is outsourced or part of the organisation's own infrastructure, will have spent the 'wrong' amount of money on it.

The higher and more immediate the availability of DR resources, the more expensive the service; it is not unheard of for organisations to be paying for availability that they don't actually need. The opposite of this is even more common, but that means that the risk in question is not actually being managed appropriately.

An example of where unnecessary availability is sometimes being paid for is work space, often called 'work area recovery'. A typical arrangement is to pay an annual fee for the right to use a certain number of 'seats' in a recovery facility at very short notice. It should be noted that, in virtually every case, this right is contractually subject to availability.

There are, however, many serviced office facilities which could probably fulfil the same purpose. Whilst a specific facility is less likely to be available at the time required, the breadth of provision may represent a similar net probability of availability, without the need to pay an annual fee.

There are, of course, other benefits associated with dedicated recovery facilities, such as 24-hour access; determining the strategy should take all these factors into account.

In business sectors such as manufacturing, where alternative operating facilities are rarely available, the strategy might focus on other ways of satisfying customers' requirements and, most importantly, meeting their expectations.

### *Business continuity planning*

Whilst this is the 'pivotal' component of the BCMS, it is arguably the simplest.

The business continuity plan (BCP) is the tool that is used to manage the response to, and recovery from, an incident or other significant business interruption.

Other terms in current use, which all describe the same thing include 'crisis management plan', 'disaster recovery plan' and 'incident management plan'.

### *What the BCP should include*

**Business continuity organisation** – the team or structure of teams that direct, lead and implement the response and recovery actions. A common term for the top level team is the 'crisis management team' (CMT). The CMT should comprise the most appropriate people to make decisions about response actions and to ensure they are implemented in the most effective way.

There can be no 'standard' CMT since every organisation is unique. It is, however, usually productive to identify specific roles and responsibilities. Simply making a list of names is unlikely to be a sufficiently robust approach as it is then impossible to establish whether the team has sufficient collective knowledge and capability to handle the range of possible issues.

It is also important to identify deputies for these roles, not only for the obvious reasons, but also to establish weaknesses (single points of failure) such as the possibility of one person performing several roles.

**Scenario-based plans** – more detailed plans designed to respond to a number of reasonably broad scenarios. Some incidents, such as fire, are site-specific whereas others, such as a flu pandemic would probably affect the entire organisation. Most importantly, the response would vary, depending upon what has happened.

The trick is to identify a relatively small number of broader scenarios for types of incident which would require similar responses. These might include:

- major site or premises incidents
- denial of access
- information and communications system failures
- supply chain failures
- pandemic flu
- loss of human resource.

These more specific 'sub-plans' enable the CMT to focus on a more relevant response, saving time and eliminating unnecessary activity.

**Procedures** – the more detailed information about how to implement response and recovery actions.

These should include at least:

- health and safety
- welfare
- security of facilities and information
- invocation and implementation of alternative resources
- resumption of business processes or activities
- internal and external communication including media handling.

**Contact information** – including that for employees, customers, key suppliers and particularly recovery service providers.

**Record forms** – an incident log should be kept to support proper accountability and to inform the review and improvement of the BCP and the BCMS.

The BCP should be accessible to all those who will need to use it in the event of activation, so distribution and control of the set of documents which comprise the plan are important elements of the BCMS. Just as the BCP is pivotal, having the wrong version of it when needed could be disastrous.

The implementation of ISO22301 naturally demands a document control system. Because of the widespread practice of electronic document distribution in virtually every organisation, the system must take into account the possibility that some managers may inadvertently refer to an old version of some, or all, of the plan.

### *Exercising*

It will be obvious to virtually everyone that incident response arrangements need to be tested from time to time since, with luck, they will rarely be deployed in a real incident.

The BCMS must include a schedule and plan for conducting exercises in a variety of scenarios in order to prove, as far as is practicable, the organisation's preparedness and ability to operate its own response procedures.

Running an exercise once or twice a year is quite typical.

### 9 Performance Evaluation - determining and documenting arrangements for:

- Monitoring, measurement, analysis and evaluation
- Internal audit
- Management review

BS25999 stated the need for maintenance; essentially making sure that arrangements and their plans are updated from time to time as things around them change. ISO22301 approaches this a little differently by saying that the organisation should decide what needs to be monitored, measured and evaluated as well as the requirement for evaluation of BC procedures. So essentially the organisation must evaluate whatever parts of the BCMS it decides should be measured as well as BC Procedures, which includes BCPs.

Every organisation changes continuously, some more than others, but it is vital that something such as the BCP, that is used irregularly if at all, is updated regularly to reflect organisational change.

Essentially, there are three ways that the BCMS should be kept up to date:

- Internal audit and management review – an approach applied to the vast majority of management systems, by which the BCMS is tested 'intellectually' to identify changes in the organisation as a whole and the resulting necessary amendments to the BCMS and, particularly, the BCP.
- Following a test, exercise or rehearsal – whilst these do cost money, some form of exercise that includes people within the organisation and tests the logic, sequence or timescales within the BCP, should be carried out with some regularity.
- Following a real activation – there can be no better test of the adequacy of a BCP than this!

All of these approaches should be set out in a maintenance plan as part of the BCMS. The standard calls for evidence of systems which ensure that all three approaches are used, and that both the BCP and the BCMS itself are reviewed and continuously improved along the lines of a quality management system compliant with ISO9000.

Once again, the contingent nature of BCM brings added challenges to this task. Very often, people who are not necessarily in the core BCM team will be asked to update a particular piece of information, or verify that it is correct.

This is where the Business Continuity Committee can help, perhaps making the timely completion of review and updating tasks a key performance indicator for the organisation, and reporting upon it at board level.

## 10 Improvement - establishing procedures for:

- Non conformance identification, reporting and consequence control
- Corrective actions (system changes)
- Continual improvement

This section is short and simple, and requires a documented system for recording when something goes wrong, or could go wrong, as well as for processing the required changes to eliminate future occurrences.

Just like its predecessor BS25999, ISO22301 says little about the requirements for continual improvement except that it should take place. Essentially it is for the organisation to say what constitutes continual improvement and then provide the evidence that it is being done. This may be as simple as saying, for example, that where a non-conformity is found, the corrective action will be reviewed for application across the BCMS, as opposed to applying it only to whatever went wrong.

### Assurance

In most organisations, the directors (or their equivalent) may assume that the BCP is fit for purpose but, unless they have valid, current evidence to that effect, they could, at least technically, be found to be negligent.

Whilst not a formal requirement of ISO22301, the BCMS should include robust arrangements under which the Business Continuity Committee, or its equivalent, reports to the board as to the adequacy and fitness for purpose of the business continuity plan, based upon the BCMS itself.

Ideally, business continuity or operational risk management should be a standing agenda item for the board or governing body of any organisation and assurance reporting could also be one of the BCM objectives stated in the policy.

# CHAPTER 5: CERTIFICATION

As with many other management system standards, there is a scheme that can be used by organisations to demonstrate their compliance with the new international standard for business continuity management.

The certification process involves an external audit conducted by an accredited external certification body.

Certification schemes exist for a number of management system standards such as ISO9001 and ISO27001. Accredited certification schemes are managed in the UK by the United Kingdom Accreditation Service (UKAS) and it would generally be unwise to secure certification from a 'certification body' that is not accredited by UKAS, or by another national accreditation body.

At the time of writing, the certification process is very much in transition; November 2012 being the official cut-off date for BS25999, however, if experience with the previous standard is anything of an indicator, it is extremely likely that certification will mature quickly and at least all of the certification bodies offering BS25999 will also offer ISO22301. Currently some are offering the new standard; however, the UKAS web-site indicates that BS25999 remains available for certification until 31st May 2014.

The certification process involves two visits by the certification auditors, usually about six weeks apart, though this could easily be significantly longer.

The first visit is likely to include:

- Assessment of the design and definition of the management system, to verify that it conforms with certification requirements such as the assessment standard(s) and certification scope.

- Assessment of the organisation's governance arrangements and the processes for assessment of risk, internal audit and management review.
- Confirmation of the contractual arrangements, including definition of approval scope, as well as the planning, logistics, sampling, etc., that will be used during the second visit.

The second visit will comprise a comprehensive assessment of the implementation of the BCMS to verify conformity with certification requirements such as the assessment standard(s) and certification scope.

The success of the assessment is likely to hinge significantly upon the comprehensiveness of evidence that all the requirements of the standard (ISO22301) are met by the BCMS and are being met in practice.

# CHAPTER 6: TERMINOLOGY

The following definitions[1] are, unless otherwise specified, taken from ISO22301:2012. A number of the definitions are further supplemented by notes, and the reader should turn to a copy of the standard itself for that information.

**Activity** – process or set of processes undertaken by an organisation (or on its behalf) that produces or supports one or more products or services.

**Audit** – systematic, independent and documented process for obtaining audit evidence and evaluating it objectively to determine the extent to which the audit criteria are fulfilled.

**Business continuity** – capability of the organisation to continue delivery of products or services at acceptable predefined levels following a disruptive incident.

**Business continuity management (BCM)** – holistic management process that identifies potential threats to an organisation and the impacts to business operations that those threats, if realised, might cause; and which provides a framework for building organisational resilience with the capability of an effective response that safeguards the interests of its key stakeholders, reputation, brand and value-creating activities.

**Business continuity management system (BCMS)** – part of the overall management system that establishes, implements, operates, monitors, reviews, maintains and improves business continuity.

---

[1] *Business Continuity and BS25999: A Combined Glossary* (ITGP, 2008) contains a comprehensive glossary of relevant terms from the world of business continuity and disaster recovery.

**Business continuity plan (BCP)** – documented procedures that guide organisations to respond, recover, resume and restore to a pre-defined level of operation following disruption.

**Business continuity programme** – ongoing management and governance process supported by top management and appropriately resourced to implement and maintain business continuity management.

**Business impact analysis (BIA)** – process of analysing activities and the effect that a business disruption might have upon them.

**Competence** – ability to apply knowledge and skills to achieve intended results.

**Conformity** – fulfilment of a requirement.

**Continual improvement** – recurring activity to enhance performance.

**Correction** – action to eliminate a detected non-conformity.

**Corrective action** – action to eliminate the cause of a non-conformity and to prevent recurrence.

**Document** – information and its supporting medium.

**Documented information** – information required to be controlled and maintained by an organisation and the medium on which it is contained.

**Effectiveness** – extent to which planned activities are realised and planned results achieved.

**Event** – occurrence or change of a particular set of circumstances.

**Exercise** – process to train for, assess, practice and improve performance in an organisation.

**Incident** – situation that might be, or could lead to, a business disruption, loss, emergency or crisis.

**Infrastructure** – system of facilities, equipment and services needed for the operation of an organisation.

**Interested party stakeholder** – person or organisation that can affect, be affected by, or perceive themselves to be affected by a decision or activity.

**Internal audit** – audit conducted by, or on behalf of, the organisation itself for management review and other internal purposes, and which might form the basis for an organisation's self-declaration of conformity.

**Invocation** – act of declaring that an organisation's business continuity plan needs to be put into effect in order to continue delivery of key products or services.

**Management system** – set of interrelated or interacting elements of an organisation to establish policies and objectives, and processes to achieve those objectives.

**Maximum acceptable outage (MAO)** – time it would take for adverse impacts, which might arise as a result of not providing a product/service or performing an activity, to become unacceptable.

**Maximum tolerable period of disruption** – time it would take for adverse impacts, which might arise as a result of not providing a product/service or performing an activity, to become unacceptable.

**Measurement** – process to determine a value.

**Minimum business continuity objective (MBCO)** – minimum level of service and/or products that is acceptable to the organisation to achieve its business objectives during a disruption.

**Monitoring** – determining the status of a system, a process or an activity.

**Mutual aid agreement** – pre-arranged understanding between two or more entities to render assistance to each other.

**Non-conformity** – non-fulfilment of a requirement.

**Objective** – result to be achieved.

**Organisation** – person or group of people that has its own functions with responsibilities, authorities and relationships to achieve its objectives.

**Outsource (verb)** – make an arrangement where an external organisation performs part of an organisation's function or process.

**Performance** – measurable result.

**Performance evaluation** – process of determining measurable results.

**Personnel** – people working for and under the control of the organisation.

**Policy** – intentions and direction of an organisation as formally expressed by its top management.

**Procedure** – specified way to carry out an activity or process.
**Process** – set of interrelated or interacting activities, which transforms inputs into outputs.

**Products and services** – beneficial outcomes provided by an organisation to its customers, recipients and interested parties, e.g. manufactured items, car insurance, regulatory compliance and community nursing.

**Prioritised activities** – activities to which priority must be given following an incident in order to mitigate impacts.

**Record** – statement of results achieved or evidence of activities performed.

**Recovery point objective (RPO)** – point to which information used by an activity must be restored to enable the activity to operate on resumption.

**Recovery time objective (RTO)** – period of time following an incident within which:

- Product or service must be resumed, or
- Activity must be resumed, or
- Resources must be recovered

**Requirement** – need or expectation that is stated, generally implied or obligatory.

**Resources** – all assets, people, skills, information, technology (including plant and equipment), premises, and supplies and information (whether electronic or not) that an organisation has to have available to use, when needed, in order to operate and meet its objectives.

**Risk** – effect of uncertainty on objectives.

**Risk appetite** – amount and type of risk that an organisation is willing to pursue or retain.

**Risk assessment** – overall process of risk identification, risk analysis and risk evaluation.

**Risk management** – coordinated activities to direct and control an organisation with regard to risk.

**Testing** – procedure for evaluation; a means of determining the presence, quality or veracity of something.

**Top management** – person or group of people who direct and control an organisation at the highest level.

**Verification** – confirmation, through the provision of evidence, that specified requirements have been fulfilled.

**Work environment** – set of conditions under which work is performed.